THE GO GO GAZELLE

Monet Love-Peterson

Illustrated By: Hadiamir Farhan

Design Copyright@2021 by Danyel Ayers

Illustrated By: Hadiamir Farhan

All rights reserved. No part of this publication may be reproduced, stored in a retrieval system or transmitted in any form or by any means, electronic, mechanical, photocopying, recording, or otherwise, without the prior permission of the publisher.

Printed in the Unted States of America
Lulu Press, Morrisville, NC

First time printing: July 2021

ISBN: **978-1-7362209-3-1**

To the kindest son in the world, my son Abiy. Thank you for opening your heart to your family and loved ones. You are patient and you know how to endure. Your endurance as a runner is unmatched. It blesses me when I know that you stop to help others along your life's journey even when it's inconvenient. No man is an island and we need one another. God has been patient with you and has proven to you that he loves you. Never stop helping those in need. You are loving God each time you are patient and give of yourself to others.

Love you Always & Forever
Mom

The fit and fast gazelle was patient at best,
He was running his race and so full of zest.

He watches the sun,
A true champion
Louds rise over the mountains,
Horizon kisses while he runs.

On his path, about his day
He heard a hurting pained voice say,
Can you help me? Can you try?
Give me a ride, so I can survive!

An injured mountain goat kept whining
ain from his leg came through the shining.
The bright shining of the sun
Abiy wanted to finish his run.
But how could he go on and ignore,
The painful shrills of this roar.

Abiy gave the goat a ride
and kept moving at a great stride.
He could stop and help him out
just keep running without a doubt.

Enjoying his run, he was half-way there.
He heard the pants of a quiet pair
A pair of little baby zebras,
Very cute but barely breathing.
They asked Abiy to lead them to water
He wanted to finish so this was a tall order.

biy thought, this may be too much?
But he threw them on his back
They were a cute little bunch.

Yeah, his load was quite heavy,
but the sunshine kept him focused and steady.
Steady load and steady pace,
Determined to come in first place.

He was almost at the finish line.
opping to help, he lost track of time.
He kept focused, "I'm almost there!"
The finished line was just a glare.

Abiy collapsed just before the end,
That's when his heavy load jumped right in.
The mountain goat and two zebras,
Carried him over so he could reach,
Reach his destination and finish
Helping others was his life mission.

So while you're running your own race,
Never go too fast or turn your face.
Don't turn from those who may need you.
God will use you so remain true.

We are all a connected village.
Each one is a reflection of God's image.
Everyone is our sister and brother.
Never forget we need one another.

www.ingramcontent.com/pod-product-compliance
Lightning Source LLC
Chambersburg PA
CBHW061406160426
42813CB00088B/2715